To David

Many Thanks for taking
us around England.

Arnold R.

Aug / 1992.

1. 3rd Troop 'C' Squadron Chieftain Mk II driven by Trooper Paul Milnes on Salisbury Plain, 1969.

2. Visit by HRH The Princess Margaret to Happy Valley, Cyprus, 11 November 1976, where she reviewed the 2nd Troop C Squadron. The princess shows an interest in Trooper Anderson's scout car. In attendance are Lieutenant-Colonel R H G McCarthy, Major C A G Wells and Her Royal Highness's equerry.

The 15th/19th The King's Royal Hussars

A Pictorial History

3. Machine Gun Troop, Egypt 1927.

Ralph Thompson

First published in 1989 by
Quoin Publishing Limited
The Barn
36a North Road
Kirkburton
Huddersfield
West Yorkshire HD8 0RH

© 1989 Text and photographs The 15th/19th The King's Royal Hussars'
Regimental Museum, Fenham Barracks, Fenham, Newcastle-Upon-Tyne

Printed and bound in the United Kingdom by
Netherwood Dalton & Co Ltd, Huddersfield

ISBN: 1-85563-004-4

4. Commanders view from a Chieftain tank of a Centurion in the open. Salisbury Plain 1969.

Introduction

The 15th/19th The King's Royal Hussars covers the period from the amalgamation of the 15th The King's Hussars and the 19th Queen Alexandra's Own Hussars, to the modern regiment of the 1980s. The book is not intended as a blow by blow account of the last eighty years, that ground has been well covered before, but is an attempt to recreate the feel and atmosphere of service life whether in India in the 1930s, Malaya in the 1950s, or in Germany, Northern Ireland, Hong Kong, or Cyprus.

The photographs form the core of the book and are used to tell the story of the men, animals and machines through the eyes of contemporary photographers rather than by looking back with hindsight. The text is intended to compliment and amplify the photographs, and to fill in the parts that for which no photographs exist. Each photograph is well worth careful study as much interesting detail lurks in the background. For the military historian and modeler alike a wealth of new information can be gleaned from these pages, as virtually none of these images have been published before.

5. Command Troop manning perimeter defences on exercise Western Venture in the Moselle, 1983.

15th The King's Hussars

The regiment was formed in 1922 by the amalgamation of the 15th The King's Hussars and the 19th (Queen Alexandra's Own Royal) Hussars. The 15th Hussars were raised in March 1759 by Major General George Augustus Eliott and known as 15th (or Light) Regiment of Dragoons and at times 'Eliott's Light Horse'. At the time, there happened to be a strike of journeymen tailors, many of whom enlisted in the newly formed Regiment, thus the nickname of "The Tabs" was adopted and is continued in the Regimental Newspaper, the Tab. The regiment, now known as the 19th Hussars, was originally raised as the 23rd Light Dragoons in 1781 when the directors of the East India Company applied to the Crown for the loan of a cavalry regiment to serve in India. In 1786 the 23rd were redesignated 19th Light Dragoons.

The 15th Hussars saw service in the Seven Years War. At the Battle of Emsdorf 1760, the regiment successfully charged home several times and received the surrender of five French battalions. This became the regiment's first battle honour. In 1765 George III inspected the regiment at Hyde Park and, struck by their appearance, he conferred on them the title of "15th (or King's) Light Dragoons". By 1794 the French Revolutionary War had broken out and the regiment was involved in an engagement at Villers-en-Cauchies. Charging home, the 15th scattered six French infantry battalions formed in squares and saved the Emperor of Austria from imminent defeat. The Austrian royal pattern gold lace was granted to the regiment as a result, and is still worn by officers on their uniforms today.

In 1807 the regiment was renamed 15th (King's) Hussars and in 1808 embarked with Sir John Moore's force for the Peninsular War. On 21st December 1808 at the town of Sahagun the 15th charged two regiments of French cavalry, utterly routing them at a cost of two lives and twenty-three wounded. This engagement has become the regiment's main battle honour. In 1813 the 15th Hussars and the 51st Regiment, now the 2nd Battalion Light Infantry, were involved in an incident whilst fording the River Esla. The river was swollen, and many men and horses were swept away by the current. However, some of the 51st were saved by clinging to the stirrups of the Hussars. This incident has never been forgotten by either regiment and is celebrated annually whenever possible.

At Waterloo two years later, the 15th were involved in several charges in the area of Hougomont Farm. From 1816 onwards the regiment was on home duty in England and Ireland, and then in 1839 embarked for India. After completing their tour they returned to England in 1854, and did not see service in either the Crimea or the Indian Mutiny. In 1869 the 15th left England for their second tour of India and took part in the Second Afghan War. During the Boer War they were firstly in England and subsequently in India for a third tour before returning to Aldershot in 1913.

6. Dublin 1921. 15th Hussars picquet and guard pose for the camera prior to going on duty. Sergeant C Garforth VC is seated on the second row fifth from the left.

19th (Queen Alexandra's Own) Royal Hussars

The story of the 19th (Queen Alexandra's Own Royal) Hussars is very different. Until 1914 they had never set foot in Europe, all their honours being won in Asia, Africa and America. On 24th September 1781 Sir John Burgoyne was directed to raise a regiment of Light Dragoons. A large draft of officers, non-commissioned officers and men from the 15th Hussars were sent to make up the new regiment.

In 1782 the 19th landed in India, earning their name "Terrors of the East" in the Mahratta War that followed. At the battle of Assaye, 1803, the "bloodiest battle the Duke of Wellington had ever known", the Regiment was granted a Battle Honour, and in 1807, Royal assent was given for the Elephant superscribed 'Assaye' to be used in the colours and appointments of the 19th Light Dragoons. This is still worn on the Regimental belt today.

In 1806 the 19th Hussars relieved His Majesty's 69th Regiment (2nd Battalion The Welsh Regiment) at the mutiny at Velore. In October 1806 the regiment sailed to England and then to Canada in 1813. In 1821 the regiment was disbanded. In May 1861 the 1st Bengal European Light Cavalry (raised in 1858 by the East India Company) was redesignated 19th Light Dragoons, and in August of the same year, redesignated 19th Hussars. By this time, the 19th Hussars had gained the nickname "The Dumpies", the reason being that the Government would only allow the East India Company to recruit men up to the height of five feet four inches. The Royal Army had priority on men above this height. In 1882 the regiment embarked for Egypt and then the Sudan and were later granted the title "Princess of Wales Own" for their services. At the outbreak of the Boer War the regiment sailed for South Africa and was besieged at Ladysmith, returning to England in 1903.

During the First World War both regiments served on the Western Front as Divisional Cavalry and had a mainly dismounted role. After amalgamation in 1922 the regiment served in Egypt and India until returning to England in 1934. By 1939 the regiment had been equipped with light tanks and carriers and served in the opening campaign in Belgium before withdrawing through Dunkirk. For the next four years the regiment was in England. The regiment landed in Europe in August 1944, and advanced from Normandy to the Baltic, reaching the Elbe by the end of the war. Since 1946 the regiment has served in Germany, Palestine, Egypt, Cyprus, Transjordan, the Sudan, the Arabian Peninsular, Libya, Hong Kong, Canada and Northern Ireland. Tours in Germany have included Munster (1961-68), Fallingbostel (1970-74), Paderborn (1977-84) and currently Detmold from 1986.

BAND, 19TH (Q.A.O.) ROYAL HUSSARS.
MUTTRA—INDIA, 1920.

B. SQUADRON 19TH (Q·A·O) ROYAL HUSSARS
MUTTRA — INDIA, 1920.

CORPORALS MESS 19TH (Q·A·O) ROYAL HUSSARS.
MUTTRA — INDIA, 1920.

10-15. Standing on the banks of the Jumna River, Muttra City, India. This was the last overseas posting for the 19th Hussars before the Regiment was disbanded. It was perhaps fitting as the Regiment's direct line of descent went back to the 1st Bengal European Light Cavalry, raised at Allahabad in July 1858. The photograph at bottom left is of one of the barrack blocks.

Muttra Cup

Back to the days of the British Raj and the Muttra Cup, a pig-sticking competition inaugurated in 1913 by the Inniskilling Dragoons and contested only twice before the outbreak of the Great War.

In December 1919 the 19th Hussars returned to India and it was decided that the cup should be resurrected as soon as possible to be played for by teams of three from regiments and tent clubs, the object of the exercise being the death of a pig, the team securing the greatest number of kills in a given number of runs, being the winner.

The first postwar competition was a three-day event held in 1921; the nine teams taking part were 'D' Battery RHA; 21st East of India Lancers; 7th Lancers; 'C' Battery RHA; The Kharwa Tent Club; HH The Maharaja of Bharatpur's team; and three teams fielded by the 19th Hussars.

The competition took place just north of Khairet, spectators being taken by lorry to Farah, where they boarded elephants so that they could keep up with the chase. The pigs were soon on the move and the 21st Lancers got away first but lost their intended victim in the palm jungle whilst 'C' Battery and 19th Hussars 'C' soon lost their pigs after only a short run when their quarry ran into thick grass. At the end of the first day the 7th Lancers were in the lead with two pigs, whilst 'C' Battery, 'D' Battery and 19th Hussars 'B' had one pig each — the other teams failed to score.

The second day's competition took place near Jundipur. Two heats were held on the nullahs above the river bed and two other heats took place across the river. The pig soon began to break cover running in all directions. Chaos ensued with pigs and riders going in all directions, crossing and recrossing and charging each other end on amidst shouts of "Get out of the way! That's my pig!" but a run by the 19th Hussars 'B' and one by 'C' Battery were disqualified by the umpire for using beaters to head off their pigs.

After tiffin the north island was beaten but the pig refused to break cover and no team had a run until the top of the nullahs overlooking Koila Jhil were reached. The bag for the day was nine boars and three sows. The only team still to score was 19th Hussars 'C' which comprised Mr Byass, Mr Low and Mr Powell.

On the third day it was decided that the cup should be given to the winners of the best of three runs; in the case of a tie, teams would continue running until all but one had failed to kill their pig. The chase started near Samoli, heading southwards. The three teams left in the competition, 19th Hussars 'B' team; 7th Hussars and 'C' Battery RHA started together but it was the latter that got away quickly chasing a heavy boar into open country where they killed him. Many more pigs broke cover but headed into high grass, though the 7th Hussars eventually succeeded heading a sow off into the nullahs where a good run ended in a kill.

The 19th Hussars had had little sport but finally got away after a small boar. Captain Selby Lowndes gave chase but unfortunately for him his team mates (Captain Tremayne and Mr Heber Percy) never saw the pig which was lost over very difficult country. On returning from this failure to the line, a boar suddenly broke cover and the 19th gave chase.

At the same time 'C' Battery were sent after a sow which they hunted well through thick grass but finally lost. Soon after returning to the line, they were put on to a good boar which turned left into thick grass where they lost him, albeit for a short while before he once more broke cover and the chase was taken up again. The 7th Hussars were immediately sent into a small patch of jhow, where several boar had been spotted, and almost at once a large boar broke and headed straight towards the elephants, hotly pursued by Captain Chandos Pole. Unfortunately the captain fell heavily but Major Thornton and Captain Weatherall took over and made a kill some distance behind the line after a good hunt.

The 19th Hussars were then taken to the same jhow where they succeeded in obtaining a kill. Operations then ceased and a very late tiffin was taken. The 7th and 19th were level with two pigs each but the 7th had a run in hand so some grass about 400 yards from the tiffin bagh was beaten and a large boar broke cover. The 7th gave chase and after a good hunt succeeded in obtaining a kill and winning the cup. The bag for the day was five boars and one sow; the total for the three days being twenty-three pigs.

16. Contestants, Mem Sahibs and helpers for the 1921 Muttra Cup.

17. 1921 Muttra Cup. The flag elephant takes a well earned rest.

18. HH the Maharaja of Bharatpur (*centre*) and his team with their one and only kill of the competition.

19. Muttra Cup, 1921. At 6.45am on Monday 28 March, the first day of the competition, competitors and spectators were taken by lorry from the 19th Hussars depot to the horse camp at Barari. From here the competitors rode the four miles to the palm jungle at Goria whilst the spectators were taken by lorry to Farah, where they mounted elephants and headed for the thick jungle just north of Khairet. There were thirteen elephants, ten having been lent by HH the Maharaja of Bharatpur and three by Mr Allan Freemantle. On the first day only five pigs were killed; the 7th Hussars got two whilst 'D' Battery RHA, 'C' Battery RHA and the 19th Hussars 'B' team scored one each. The 21st (E of I) Lancers, Kharwa Tent Club, 19th Hussars 'A' and 'C' teams and the Bharatpur team all failed to score.

20. The last mounted parade of the 19th Hussars was held at Muttra in 1921.

21. Following the disbandment of the regiment, a contingent of 121 NCOs and men is photographed leaving Muttra for Risalpur where they were to join the 18th Hussars. Most of the officers and men of the 19th were transferred to other regiments then serving in India. However, a small number returned to England with Lieutenant-Colonel Parsons. On 11 April 1922, Army Order No 133 was published. His Majesty the King was graciously pleased to approve the reconstitution of four recently disbanded cavalry regiments (the 5th Royal Irish Lancers, 19th Royal Hussars, 20th Hussars and 21st Lancers) which were then to be merged with other units. As a whole the establishment of the regular cavalry was to be one regiment of Household Cavalry and eight regiments of the line. The 1st and 2nd Life Guards were merged into one regiment of four squadrons. The 19th were merged with the 15th (The King's) Hussars to form the 15th/19th Hussars. As 'C' Squadron of the new regiment, the 19th retained their own insignia and traditions.

23. Lieutenant-Colonel Parsons says farewell to the last members of the 19th Hussars, Tidworth, England, November 1921. Five months later, dispersed members of the regiment were brought back together to reform the unit for the amalgamation with the 15th (The King's) Hussars

24. Asaye Barracks, Tidworth. The amalgamated regiment on parade. The regiment remained at Tidworth until 11 January 1924, when it embarked for Egypt, arriving at Port Said fourteen days later. Until December 1926 the regiment was based at Helmieh with detachments at Sidi Bishr and Mena Camp.

25. The 15th/19th hold their very own Chelsea Flower Show. The Guard Room at Helmieh Camp in 1925.

26. Not quite the set of a Rudolf Valentino picture but the camp cinema was the venue for many a silent movie star.

27. In 1927 'B' Squadron was disbanded and a machine gun squadron formed. At this time United States cavalry regiments were about to have their machine gun troops reinstated, each comprising of eight ·30-calibre Browning water-cooled machine guns, three 37mm guns and three light armoured cars mounting anti-aircraft machine guns.

28. On 14 December 1926 the regiment moved from Helmieh to Abbassia. 'C' Squadron are photographed somewhere on their desert march Abbassia-Wadi Natrum-Abbassia, a distance of 185 miles which they covered in nine days.

29. 15th/19th Hussars at the Command Searchlight Tattoo, Gezireh. Lined up for the steeplechase are (*left to right*) Lieutenant Cockayne Frith, Lieutenant-Colonel Smith Bingham, Lieutenant's Hinde, Haggas, Arnott, Agnew, Second Lieutenant Head and Captain Hambury.

30. Officers in historical costume pass the port prior to the midnight steeplechase at Gezireh.

31. "Eat your heart out Tom Mix!" The regimental vaulting team are home on the range at the Gezireh Searchlight Tattoo.

32. Abbassia Camp, 1927. Officers Mess staff in royal livery granted by George III in October 1801.

33. Corporal Shakespeare of 'C' Squadron with the winners cup for best corporal at the Egyptian Command Rifle Meeting.

34. Egypt 1924-28. 'C' Squadron mount guard.

35. Warrant officers and sergeants at Helmjeh Camp, Egypt. As can be seen the 19th Hussars senior ranks wear their own regimental badges and insignia, including the elephant toppee badge introduced in 1920.

36. The regimental band photographed in Cairo, August 1928. On 20 October the regiment sailed for India reaching Risalpur on 14 November.

37. Jamrud Fort situated at the entrance to the Khyber Pass. The two boxes jutting out from the top of the tower are machine gun posts.

38-39. Afridi tribesmen, North West Frontier, 1930.

41. Khanspur Hill Station, Murree Hills. The station was used by the regiment during the hot weather season, each squadron spending at least six weeks here where they concentrated upon musketry and dismounted drills.

40. North West Frontier tribesman, 1930.

42. Taking a breather during the march to Peshawar are members of 5 Machine Gun Troop. Whilst in India the designation of the regiment was changed in 1932 from 15th/19th Hussars to the 15th The King's Royal Hussars by Army Order 177.

43. In camp on the Frontier, 18 February 1933. The cavalry units are dispersed around the camp whilst a lorry park has been established in the centre by the road. The artillery contingent of eight guns is located in the top corner. *Instruments are from left to right:* Clock, Camera specification, direction of sun, level around the fuselage axis, level around the wing axis, photograph number and altimeter.

44. Further up the Frontier, 26 February 1933. The brigade is camped around a small fort. On 21 December 1933, Army Order 207 changed the title of the regiment to the 15th/19th The King's Royal Hussars. On this photograph the direction of the sun does not show as the camera is pointing obliquely.

45. On 15 January 1934, the regiment embarked for England where it was stationed at Shorncliffe until November 1935 when it moved to Tidworth. This photograph of the regimental guard was taken at Shorncliffe (Corporal Butler is the guard commander).

46. Mechanisation looms. The regiment's motor transport section of Morris Commercial R Type lorries at Shorncliffe, 1934.

47. Austin Scouts at York in 1937. The Signal and Scout Troops were formed at Shorncliffe in 1934.

48. Signals Troop at York in 1937 equipped with 1936 built Morris 8HP cars. It was at York that the regiment underwent training for mechanisation, the last horses leaving in April 1938.

49-50. The first mechanised camp was held at Binnington near Scarborough in August 1938 where the regiment trained with the few light tanks, carriers and 15cwt trucks they had been issued with.

51. The regiment was mobilised on 1 September 1939 as Divisional Cavalry 3rd Division and equipped with Dragon light tanks, Cardon Lloyds and trucks. On 2 October the regiment embarked for France arriving at St Nazaire two days later. During 1939 the regiment was stationed at a number of places including La Plaisance, Monchy-Breton, Perenchise and Bethune. On 10 May 1940 the 15th/19th The King's Royal Hussars crossed the Belgian frontier at Herseaux (*above*) going into action later that same day.

52. A Vickers-Armstrong Light Tank rolls through Herzele, about twenty miles west of Assche, where the first and the most costly contact was made with the enemy. The Regiment was responsible for protecting the right flank of the Belgians, and for the withdrawal across the Dendre at Alost, against vastly superior numbers and equipment. The survivors also rested here on the night of 18th May.

After this action, only one squadron of fighting vehicles and crews could be mustered to cover the withdrawal of three Divisions. Attrition on the vehicles reduced the Squadron to two light tanks and seven carriers, and on the 26th May came the order to hand them over to The 5th Royal Inniskilling Dragoon Guards and reform as infantry in GHQ reserve. The squadron now comprised five troops of about 25 men armed with rifles and a few Bren guns. Marching from just inside the Belgian border at Steenwerk near Armentieres via Watou and Bergues to Dunkirk, and harassed by air attack and shelling, the squadron arrived battered and bloody but undefeated. HMS *Malcolm* evacuated the majority of the men directly from the mole at Dunkirk, returning to Dover on the 30th. So ended the regiment's spirited participation in what was to become known as the miracle of Dunkirk.

53. Entertainment inside Stalag XXIA, Schilberg, Poland. SSM J R Laing (*on the right*) was wounded and taken prisoner on 18 May 1940 at Assche, Belgium. Laing rejoined the regiment in September 1945 and was awarded the DCM. The fighting in Belgium and France cost the regiment seven officers and twenty-seven other ranks killed and six officers and a hundred other ranks taken prisoner.

54. On returning from Dunkirk the regiment was re-equipped and on 19 November 1940 was assigned to the 9th Armoured Division. After being stationed at Bovington, then Rowmarsh and Uttoxeter, the regiment moved to Rushden where it remained throughout 1941. The photograph shows 'C' Squadron Covenanter tanks led by Captain R F Daubigny, training on Dunstable Downs in September 1941.

55. HRH The Duke of Gloucester inspecting the 15th/19th The King's Royal Hussars at Spencer Park, Rushden, Northants, 15 February 1941.

56. Eindhoven, Holland, 17 September 1944, the day the regiment linked up with the American 101st Airborne Division. The photograph is of a Challenger tank of 2nd Troop, 'A' Squadron.

57. The 15th/19th The King's Royal Hussars sailed for Normandy on 14 August 1944 and were in action until the end of the war. On 17 September the regiment crossed into Belgium and took part in the advance through Holland towards Germany crossing into Reich territory on 24 February 1945. This photograph shows tanks trundling through the ruins of the German town of Cleve.

58. River crossing somewhere in Germany. The tracked vehicle sporting the star is an armoured recovery vehicle.

59. A Jagdpanzer IV/7D or hunting tank knocked out by the regiment. These were designed for the ambushing of main battle tanks. They carried an 88mm gun, heavy frontal armour and had a very low silhouette. Lacking the added complexity of a turret, they were lighter and easier to produce. A few twin gun versions were even experimented with.

60. 10 March 1945. Waiting on the outskirts of Nijmegen for transports to convey the regiment back to Louvain in Belgium where they would convert to Comets. Nijmegen bridge is in the background. On the back of the tank is Corporal Lucas MM, and in the foreground is Lieutenant Fitzpatrick.

61. Trooper Broad, 'B' Squadron prepares dinner in the squadron harbour to the south east of Nijmegen, 10 March 1945.

62. 95mm howitzer Cromwells of FHQ 'B' Squadron at Burgstienfurt, 31 March 1945. Powered by a V12 600hp Rolls-Royce Meteor 27 litre engine and using Christie type suspension, the Cromwell was capable of 40mph making it one of the fastest tanks of World War Two. Drive was via the rear sprockets through a five speed Merrit Brown gearbox and controlled differential, with hydraulic steering brakes.

63. Me262A-1a jet fighter abandoned by the *Luftwaffe* on the Hamburg-Lubeck autobahn which had been used as a runway. First flown operationally in April 1944 and capable of reaching 540mph, the 262 represented a quantum leap in fighter design. The detached rearming panels show the link and case ejector chutes for the portside 30mm cannon; four were carried with a total of 360 rounds. It was also capable of carrying two 551 pound bombs. These were used in an endeavour to close the bridge at Nijmegen. Spitfire XIVs and Tempest Vs on standing patrols, umbrella and radial anti-aircraft barrages all proved incapable of stopping the attacks, although in practice they achieved little more than nuisance value.

64. Is this the regiment's flying club? Members of 'B' Squadron inspect the Me262A-1a.

65. 5-10 May 1945. 'C' Squadron booty on display at Schlamersdorf.

66. 10 May 1945. The fighting is over so its time for a clean up. 'B' Squadron at Satrup. The tanks are Comets. Mechanically similar to the Cromwell and with improved Christie suspension, 17-pdr gun and all welded armour, they were developed in 1944 and saw service in the latter stages of the war.

67. Schleswig-Holstein, May 1945. Captain Weatherby MC sitting on top of a Humber scout car leads in a group of displaced persons, thought to be Yugoslavs who had fought on the German side.

68. 'B' Squadron officers, Germany 1945. Lieutenant S R M Frazer, Captain J S Sutherland, Lieutenant R F Eyles, Captain The Earl of Harrington, Major The Lord Rathdonnell MC and Captain C N Weatherby MC.

69-71. After the German surrender, the Third Reich carried on in the form of the Dönitz government in Flensburg, where armed German soldiers formed the garrison and the Swastika flag continued to fly. There was an outside chance that the Flensburg government might have been tolerated as a central German authority, but the regime exceeded itself when Field Marshal Busch announced that he was assuming full command in Schleswig-Holstein, and Dönitz publicly stated that the Western Allies should join Germany in stopping Communism from spreading into Europe. On 23 May, Dönitz, Jodl and von Friedeburg were arrested and their government dissolved, the 15th/19th being one of the units sent into Flensburg to carry out the task. *Above left:* The adjutants driver Trooper Nunns and one of the cars "commandeered" by the regiment at Flensburg. *Above right:* The CO's new staff car, a Mercedes. If this was the car that Dönitz had used at Flensburg, then its previous owner was non other than Adolf Hitler! *Left:* Also appropriated by the regiment were 122 horses among which were three international show jumpers, *Memphis, Zirkel* and *Turban*; together with these beautiful carriage horses which had been a gift to von Ribbentrop from Admiral Horthy. In May 1945, the stables, along with the *Wehrmacht* grooms, took on the title of 'D' Squadron and were placed under the command of Captain J Prestwich.

72. *Below:* 'B' Squadron search the village of Ohe for Heinrich Himmler, but he had already fled.

73. The regimental gymkhana and sports meeting held near Kappeln on 8 September 1945, the regiment's last day in Germany. Major The Lord Rathdonnell MC is on the left.

74. Major The Lord Rathdonnell MC at the regimental gymkhana. On the 9th September the regiment left Germany for Ath in Belgium where they remained until 10 October when they began their travels to Egypt and the Canal Zone.

75. 'B' Squadron tank crew. Corporal M Lucas (*second left*) was awarded the MM for his actions on 10 September 1944. The tank in which he was operator was hit and the commander, Captain Agnew, was wounded. Corporal Lucas managed to get the captain out of the tank and then went back to attend to the rest of the crew. Captain Agnew, being dazed, started to crawl toward the enemy but Corporal Lucas succeeded in retrieving him whilst under fire. After handing Captain Agnew over to the MO, Lucas returned to his tank and took over command.

76. Lieutenant Beastall of 'C' Squadron with a GMC armoured truck, one of many types of vehicles issued to the regiment in Palestine in 1946. The APC is Canadian with 8 seat bodywork by the Hamilton Bridge Company, based on a 15cwt General Motors chassis and powered by a 100bhp engine. About 4,000 were built between 1943 and 1944.

77. 'C' Squadron Sherman tanks in the Sinai Desert, 1946.

78-79. Night firing exercise for the benefit of the Egyptian Army, 1947.

80-82. On arriving in the Canal Zone in October 1945 the regiment was assigned to the 3rd Infantry Division. Before the end of the year the regiment was posted to Palestine on security duties returning to Egypt in 1947. A second spell of security duty in Palestine was followed by a return to Egypt where 'C' Squadron was to remain to run down whilst the rest of the regiment moved to the Sudan with the 1st Infantry Division. *Above left:* En route to the Sudan. After four days on board ship from Suez to Port Sudan, the regiment's vehicles are loaded on railway flat cars for the twenty-four hour journey to Khartoum, November 1947. *Left:* A Troop of 'A' Squadron at camp Kilo 5, Khartoum, 1948. The 15th/19th was the first cavalry regiment to be stationed in the Sudan since the 21st Lancers fought the Battle of Omdurman in 1898. *Above:* Jock Lennox, 3rd Troop, 'B' Squadron at North Barracks, Khartoum, 1948. From the Sudan, the regiment returned to England for an albeit brief stay before returning to Germany. The regiment was based at Lubeck until 1951, then followed deployments to Rhalstedt Hamburg, Neumunster and finally Wesendorf. In 1953 the regiment joined the 7th Armoured Division and left Germany on 4 May 1954 for Colchester.

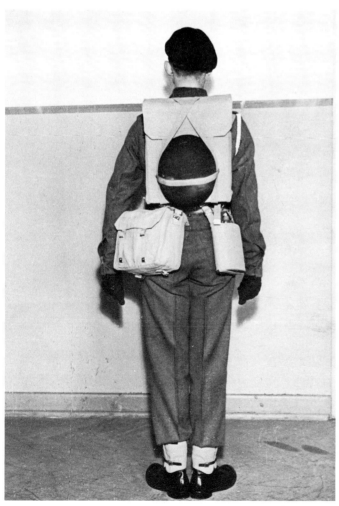

83-84. 15th/19th The King's Royal Hussars field service marching order, Lubeck, Germany, 1949.

85. On 11 July 1954 the regiment arrived in Singapore on board the *Empire Clyde* and on 26 August took over operational duties from the 12th Lancers. Photograph taken at Raub, Malaya, 1954 of FHQ Troop, 'C' Squadron. *Front row left to right:* Corporal Deville, Sergeant Goodier, Major Eggleton MC, Captain Gordon-Smith MC, SSM Simmonds and Corporal Shuttleworth. *Centre row left to right:* Trooper Pritchard, Sergeant Wilson, Lance-Corporal Williams, Troopers Harbinson and Powell, Signaller Horn and Trooper Wilson. *Rear left to right:* Troopers Lawlor and Page.

86. 'C' Squadron patrol which captured a terrorist on 21 January 1955 included Troopers Allamby, Martin, Kendall, Powell, Sprigg, Jones and Corporal Conlon who was mentioned in despatches.

87. 'C' Squadron patrol getting a wounded terrorist across a fast flowing river. Second Lieutenant Campion is on the extreme right of the photograph.

88. Near Taiping, January 1956. Troopers Thompson and McIntosh and Lance-Corporal Powell take a break but need a can opener.

89. 18 December 1956. Landslide in the Cameron Highlands. The vehicle hovering over the edge is a 3 tonner. Corporal Wells and Trooper Walker 301 were killed in the accident.

90. Daimler armoured car of 5th Troop, 'A' Squadron passing the Sam Poh Tong Buddhist Temple near Ipoh, July 1956.

91-94. HQ Squadron recovering a ditched Daimler armoured car commanded by Lieutenant Mark Burns. The repair bill came to £5.17s.3d. Mark Burns later took part in the film *The Charge of the Light Brigade*, proving that he was better on four feet than four wheels!

95. Corporal P Bircham of the RHQ Troop twiddles the dials on the radio set of a Saracen Command Vehicle, Ipoh, Malaya, 1957.

96. It could be anywhere in the UK but this is in fact the Smoke Lodge in the Cameron Highlands, Malaya, 1957. Good beer, good food, discreet licensing hours.

Whilst in Malaya the regiment was based at Ipoh with detachments serving at a number of places including Raub, Taiping, Kulim, Cameron Highlands, Bikam, Kuantan and Sungei Siput. In 1955 elements of the regiment were present at the Baling Talks which were held with the communists in an attempt to resolve Malaya's troubles. On 4 June 1957, the regiment embarked on board the *Empire Orwell* disembarking at Southampton on 6 July. 'A' Squadron remained in Aden.

97. 'A' Squadron in Aden 1957. The patrol is halted at the fort at Themir on the Aden-Dhala road.

98. In January 1958 'A' Squadron rejoined the regiment which was then stationed in Northern Ireland on internal security duties. Here the 2nd Troop is on exercise during the IRA 'close season' imposed in the summer of 1958.

99-100. The Training Wing goes through its paces on the Magilligan Ranges, Northern Ireland, 1958.

101. 'B' Squadron Daimler armoured car and a Saracen APC on patrol in Northern Ireland, 1958.

102. Bi-centenary and Guidon presentation, Barnard Castle, 26 September 1959. 'B' Squadron march past.

103. HRH The Princess Margaret, Colonel in Chief of the Regiment, visiting the regimental stables, accompanied by Captain F R Meyrick and the Colonel of the Regiment, Major General Sir Robert Hinde, KBE, CB, DSO.

104. HRH The Princess Margaret with the commanding officer Lieutenant-Colonel J M Barton MC, admiring the new Guidon on display in the regimental museum

105. Members of the Regimental Association march past the saluting platform, Barnard Castle, 26 September 1959.

106. On 12 June 1959 the regiment undertook a change of role when it became the RAC's Training Regiment, a function it was to fulfil until moving to Germany in 1961. Here troopers tackle the Barnard Castle assault course.

107. Could this be the 15th/19th's answer to Beatlemania? The *Alley Cats*, Munster 1963. *Left to right:* Lance-Corporal Macbeth, Trooper Jock Munday, Trooper Hunt and Cfn. Johny Ward.

108. Munster, 26 March 1963. The band plays on during the drive past of the regiment's armour on the occasion of the visit of HRH The Princess Margaret.

109. In the words of the song "Four wheels on my wagon but I'm still rolling along . . ." A Saladin armoured car proving it's as good with four wheels as it is with six.

110. A Saladin shows its cross country capability, July 1964. The Saladin was first produced in 1958 and entered service the following year, remaining in production until 1972. It was powered by a Rolls-Royce B.80Mk6A 8-cylinder petrol engine developing 170hp at 3,750rpm and giving a top speed of 72km/h (44.72mph). The armament comprised a 76mm (3in) gun and a 7.62mm (0.30in) coaxial machine gun. Dimensions: length 5.284m (17ft 3in); height 2.19m (7ft 2in); width 2.54m (8ft 3in); weight in working order 11.59 tonnes (25,498lb); armour 8.3mm (0.32in). The 6 × 6 chassis was common to the Saracen APC and the Stalwart high-mobility load carrier. The vehicle was also fitted with run-flat tyres, and, as shown in the photograph at the top of this page, it had the capability of running despite the loss of several wheels.

111. On 1 April 1965 after a period of nineteen years, the 15th/19th The King's Royal Hussars once more became an armoured regiment. *Above:* Lance-Corporal R Dickinson and Corporal R Edwards join their French police escort for a bevy or three on the road from Munster to Larzac in the South of France, where the regiment was to take part in an exercise.

112. On 25 January 1968, the regiment returned to the UK being stationed at Tidworth (Bhurtpore Barracks). On 14 June HRH The Princess Margaret visited the regiment. Here HRH takes the salute as 'C' Squadron Centurions drive past.

113. Salisbury Plain, 14 June 1968. The regiment parades 'crews front' as HRH The Princess Margaret drives past in an open Landrover escorted by mounted outriders.

114. In August and September 1968, 'C' Squadron was stationed in the New Territories, Hong Kong. Here Centurions move through Tai Po during an exercise.

115. 'A' Squadron on exercise with the Gurkhas in the Lo Wu training area in the New Territories, Hong Kong, August 1969.

116. 'A' Squadron Centurion tank at Lo Wu. The hills in the background are in China.

117. Centurion tanks of 'A' Squadron open fire on the Lo Wu range, August 1969.

118. A Centurion and a Chieftain of The 15th/19th The King's Royal Hussars move across Salisbury Plain.

119. Lurking in the bushes. One of the regiment's Chieftain tanks on exercise on Salisbury Plain.

120. Centurion tank of 'C' Squadron, Salisbury Plain.

121. Trooper Harding from Darlington at the gun control equipment of his Centurion tank.

122. Chieftain tank using 'White light' on exercise in Germany

123. Regimental Gunnery Wing, Tidworth, 1969. The instructor is Corporal Jim Brayson, the students are Troopers Kingsland, Ditch and Cogland.

124. From July-December 1971, the regiment carried out six months operational duties in Northern Ireland though 'B' Squadron remained in Fallingbostel, Germany. *Above:* The Ardoyne, Belfast, during anti-internment riots. Trooper Stark keeps watch.

125. The regiment's KAPE Team unload a Chieftain.

126.'B' Squadron Chieftain tank, hull down on the Soltau Training Area, Germany 1974. The regiment had converted to this type of tank in 1970, the same year that the Swingfire (anti-tank missile) Troop was formed. The Chieftain first entered service with the British Army in 1967. Powered by a Leyland L60, this engine was a two stroke, turbo charged, compression ignition, multi-fuel engine, and was of an opposed piston layout with six cylinders, twelve pistons and two crankshafts, developing 750bhp at 2,250rpm. It also had the habit of sending large clouds of exhaust smoke into the air, particularly on starting up, which rather gave the game away if you were trying to hide! This 55,000kg main battle tank could reach a maximum speed of 48km/h (29.81mph). The armament comprises a 120mm (4.75in) gun capable of a sustained rate of fire of eight to ten rounds a minute for the first minute and six rounds per minute thereafter; a 7.62mm (0.3in) coaxial machine gun and a 7.62mm machine gun for anti-aircraft defence. The turret is operated by a small joystick and can be brought to bear within seconds, a 360° traverse taking about twenty seconds.

127. Stalwart high mobility load carrier crewed by Corporal Bill (Winker) Watson and Lance-Corporal Tony Hartley on exercise Yellow Tab, Germany 1974.

128. Tank 33D practices a neutral turn on the Soltau Training Area.

129. Regimental trumpeters on duty during the visit of HM Queen Elizabeth to Newcastle-upon-Tyne. *Left to right:* Corporal Taylor, Lance-Corporal Copp, Trumpet Major Alderson, Corporal Thomson and Corporal Auld.

130. Members of the old comrades association march back to camp after church parade during their visit to the regiment at Fallingbostel, September 1974.

131. From January-April 1973, 'A' and 'C' Squadrons were deployed on security duties in Northern Ireland where Lance-Corporal Stuart was awarded the MM for gallantry. In November 1974 the regiment returned to the troubled province where it was stationed at Omagh with detachments operating in St Angelo, Castlederg, Belleek, Grayvale, Kinawley, Belcoo, Lisnaskea, Cookstown and the Deanery.

Left: Lisanelly Camp, Omagh, 10 December 1974. The RSM, Jim Walls, greets General Sir Frank King, GOC Northern Ireland. Looking on is Lieutenant-Colonel Coxwell-Rogers.

132. Corporal Kingsland's section display their firepower. 'C' Squadron, Omagh.

133. "Have you ever had that sinking feeling?" Negotiating a bog in Northern Ireland.

134. 'A' Squadron on Gortin Ranges, County Tyrone.

135. 'The night owls,' Street patrol in Northern Ireland. Marty Hoyle sports a smile and a 'bone dome'.

136. Northern Ireland, 1975. Training with Carl Gustav anti-tank missiles, an extremely effective way to open suspect car boots.

137. 'It's a lot less bovver with a hovver.' A Scout helicopter recovering bogged down farm machinery. These exercises were known as 'Winning the hearts and minds of the people'.

(i). Risalpur, April 1930. A two mule powered lawnmower cutting the grass on the polo field. Note the jury rig for mules. The Mk I was pulled by Sepoys.

(ii). Pack horse inspection, Risalpur, April 1930.

(iii). Officer's Ball, The Dorchester Hotel, July 1971. HRH The Princess Margaret (Colonel-in-Chief) talking to Band Sergeant Major Carter. Also in attendance are Major-General F B Wyldbore-Smith. CB, DSO, OBE (Colonel of the Regiment) and the commanding officer, Lieutenant-Colonel J S F Murray.

(iv). 'B' Squadron take part in a United Nation's medal parade held on 1 March 1977
on the runway of Nicosia Airport, Cyprus.

(v). 'A' Squadron, Tidworth, Hants 1977. Corporal Watson (*right*)
and Trooper Foggon (*left*) get down to a little maintenance work on
a Fox armoured car.

(vi). Fox armoured car of 'A' Squadron exercising at Tidworth.
In the background is a Scorpion light tank.

(vii). August 1983. Members of 'B' Squadron take the waters during an adventure training course in the Smokey Mountains, Virginia. Shooting the rapids on the Nantahala River are Troopers Sergison, Wardle, Watson and Swann.

(viii). Champions! Burton Park, London, May 1984. The regimental football team poses for the camera. That year they won the Cavalry Cup, trouncing The Queen's Own Hussars 5-3. The Regiment also won it in 1981.

(ix)(x). Otterburn Ranges 1985. A Swingfire ATGW controlled by Corporal Steve Davies on its way to the target. *Inset:* 'Well nobody's perfect'. Swingfire and box take off with the aerodynamics of a brick toilet from Lance-Corporal O'Brien's FV438 at Larkhill in 1985. The box is supposed to stay inside the launcher – it didn't go far.

(xi). Corporal Davies' Swingfire strikes home. 'Eat your hearts out 'steam gunners''.

(xii). 'They can even do it at night without TI.' Test flights for British Aerospace 1985.

(xiii). Freedom of the city of Newcastle-upon-Tyne parade, 10 May 1986. Part of the armoured contingent trundles along Northumberland Street.

(xiv). Chieftain tank driven by Trooper Armstrong. In the commander's cupola is Sergeant Preece and alongside him is Trooper Brennan. 10 May 1986.

(xv). 'C' Squadron in combat dress and carrying Stirling sub-machine guns march past the saluting base. 10 May 1986.

(xvi). 'B' Squadron commanded by a smiling Major Forsyth marching through the city with fixed bayonets. 10 May 1986.

(xvii). Regimental Reunion Dinner held at Newcastle Civic Centre, 10 May 1986. HRH The Princess Margaret arriving with Brigadier J R D Sharpe CBE, the Colonel of the Regiment and Colonel Sir Ralph Carr Ellison TD, HML, Honorary Colonel Northumberland Hussars.

(xviii). WOI Paul Esplin in full dress uniform. Mr Esplin was Bandmaster from 1976-1986.

(xix/xx). Junior NCO's Cadre Course, Detmold, Germany 1987. *Above:* Lieutenant-Colonel D S Balmain, RSM P Milnes, the adjutant Captain M H Browell, SSGT C J Stemp and Lance-Corporal G J R Jackson who was the top student. *Below:* JNCO's 'Pass Off' Parade.

(xxi). *Opposite page top:* JNCO's Cadre Course on exercise *Rat Race* near Bad Pyrrmont, May 1987.

(xxii). *Opposite page bottom:* Lance-Corporals Hume, Jackson, Calcutt and Ball take five during exercise *Rat Race*, May 1987.

(xxiii). *Right:* JNCO's Cadre Course.

(xxiv). *Below:* Hohne Ranges 1987. 'C' Squadron preparing for a days firing.

(xxv). Awaiting their call on Hohne Ranges.

(xxvi). Captain Browell firing an LMG, Hohne Ranges, 1987.

(xxvii). Hohne Ranges 1988. 2nd Troop 'D' Squadron pose for the camera. The Troop leader,
Second-Lieutenant Curran is centre front.

(xxviii). "Tea up!" Hohne Ranges 1988.Having a brew are Sergeant Black, Lance-Corporal Davies, Corporal Ellis and
Lance-Corporal's Thompson and Johnson.

138. Inter service cooperation. The RAF lends a hand to close a border crossing.

139. Trumpet Major Bob Alderson prefers to use his personal weaponry whilst WOII Carter plays a different tune.

140. Omagh, Northern Ireland. Scout cars undergoing repair and inspection in the LAD in the capable hands of 'Q' Hockings (REME).

141. The 'MASH' Troop drive the old MO Captain Lupton out of camp tied to the top of a Saracen ambulance. The new MO Captain Spanswick stands behind him

142-144. Bomb disposal at work. *Right:* The retiring CO Lieutenant-Colonel R A Coxwell-Rogers turns the key to blow up 600lbs of recrystallised ammonium nitrate found during a search of the Greencastle area of County Tyrone by SSM John Edwards of 'B' Squadron. *Below:* The resulting explosion in a disused quarry.

145-146. Northern Ireland, 1975. A suspect car gets the before
and after treatment with the help of the *wheelbarrow*.

147. Ian Wilson (*left*) of BBC Radio Newcastle escorted by 'Super Sleuth' Peter Scott visits the aftermath of a car bomb.

148. The aftermath of yet another car bomb in Northern Ireland.

149. MT Troop, Omagh, 1975.

150. Lisanelly Camp, Omagh. 'A' Squadron on parade on Armistice Day 1975.

151. Miss 15th/19th Hussars, Joan Calder, visits the regiment's Kindergarten during her stay with the regiment in Omagh, July 1975.

152. 'Keep it up lads, we're almost at the top.' The band led by Bandmaster Evans is at the head of the RAF Association's parade through Omagh, November 1975.

153. Santa Claus and his helpers WOII Dave Gregory, Private Ricky Sangster, Corporal Dave Craig, Sergeant Ramsey Ord and Major Witheridge at Coneywarren Children's Home, Northern Ireland, 1975.

154. RSM Lofty Walls leads the cast and audience in a sing-song at the end of the regimental review, December 1975.

155. Santa Claus (looking much like 'Wor Tom') at the regimental children's Christmas party, Omagh, Northern Ireland, December 1975.

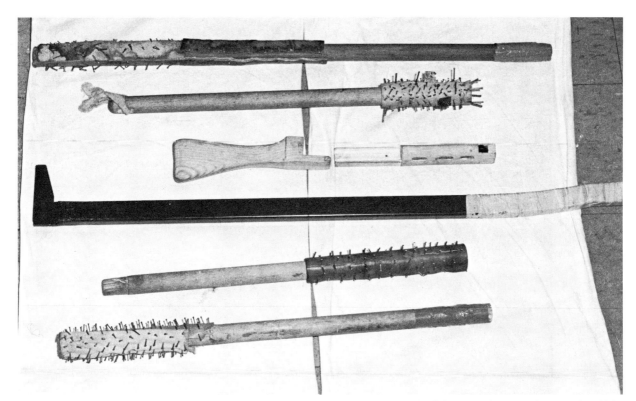

156. Exhibits from the Magilligan Prison Woodwork Society found during a search of the prison in December 1975 in which 'C' Squadron were involved.

157. Lisanelly Barracks, Omagh, 1976. Proxy bomb practice; the dogs prefer to sniff one another than anything potentially explosive!

158. Trooper Jim Armstrong training with a Carl Gustav anti-tank weapon. The Charlie G was part of 'A' Troop's weaponry during their tour of duty in Northern Ireland.

159. By mid-May 1976 the regiment had moved to Tidworth. In June 'C' Squadron was detached for duty at the Sovereign Bases in Cyprus and in September 'B' Squadron was sent to the island as part of the United Nations Force. On 11 November HRH The Princess Margaret visited 'C' Squadron in Cyprus. Photograph is of a 'C' Squadron patrol.

160. Exercise Northern Canter, 16 October 1976. Fox armoured cars of 'A' Squadron leave the south end of the Tyne Tunnel. In the first car are Corporal Humphrey and Troopers Brodie and Hall. In the second are Troopers Bolam and Skeet.

161. Peterlee detachment Army Cadet Force, badged 15th/19th The King's Royal Hussars. In the centre is Cadet Major the brother of Trooper John Major

162-163. Scotch Corner, North Yorkshire. A Fox armoured car of 'A' Squadron is brought to earth by a local hunt.

164. Otterburn Ranges, September 1977. The *Fat Ferrets* of the regiment's Guided Weapons Troop fire the last Swingfire missiles of the RAC before handing over future responsibility for them to the Royal Artillery.

165. 12 February 1977. Security duties by 'B' Squadron during the visit of Secretary-General Dr Waldheim to Cyprus. The Ferret remained in production at Daimler from 1952 to 1971, over 4,000 being built in various marks. The Mk2 was the first to be fitted with a turret which was manually operated and carried a 0.30mm Browning machine gun. The later Mk4 had larger wheels and tyres and was fitted with disc brakes.

166. 'C' Squadron Ferret scout cars lined up for the Queen's birthday parade at Episkopi, Cyprus, 1977.

167. Trooper Bri Yews of Shotton Colliery behind the wheel of a Ferret scout car, 1977.

168. Hohne Ranges, West Germany, 1978. A Scimitar of 'A' Squadron moving onto the battle run. The regiment moved to Germany in October 1977 and was stationed at Paderborn. During 1978 the 1st, 3rd and 5th Troops of 'A' Squadron were detached to Northern Ireland whilst the 2nd Troop visited Canada. The following year the 1st and 5th Troops of 'A' Squadron went to Canada whilst the 2nd Troop went to Northern Ireland. The Scimitar is one of the variants of the FV101 Scorpion combat vehicle reconnaissance developed by Alvis. The Scorpion family are powered by a Jaguar six-cylinder water-cooled petrol engine (later variants have a Perkins diesel engine) developing 190bhp and giving a maximum road speed of 80.5km/h (50mph). The Scimitar has a crew of three and is armed with a 30mm Rarden cannon.

169. Sultan Command Vehicle photographed during an exercise in West Germany in 1979.

170. Future 15th/19th Hussars? Lieutenant-Colonel E M Westropp inspects cadets of the Peterlee detachment, December 1979.

171. 'B' Squadron sport the very latest in 'Noddy Suits' for a visit by HRH The Princess Margaret. Paderborn, 20 March 1980.

172. Hohne Ranges, 1980. A Scimitar of 'A' Squadron opens up with its Rarden cannon.

173. Exercise Southern cross 1981. A worried looking Captain Webb-Bowen commanding an M113 APC driven by Trooper Thompson during training in Australia. 'C' Squadron were on an exchange visit with the 4th Australian Cavalry Regiment in Enoggera, Brisbane.

174. Whilst in Australia, 'C' Squadron, on behalf of the regiment, was presented with the South African medals of Private Herbert Wohlgemuth, 19th Hussars. The presentation was made by his grandson WOII (AQMS) Des Sykes RAEME (*on left of photograph*).

175. Paderborn, 1981. Men of the 4th Australian Cavalry Regiment are introduced to the vehicles they are to train on during their exchange visit to the regiment. Sergeant Brian Banks is in charge.

176. Paderborn. Wearing the latest in *Noddy* suits and under the watchful eye of SSM Dennis Cooper six eager lads try their luck at SMG shooting.

177. BAOR Cavalry Cup semi-final, Hohne 1981. The *Tabs* beat the 14th/20th Hussars by three goals to one. In the final they beat the 5th Inniskilling Dragoon Guards 2-1 and then went on to beat the UK finalists, the Royal Hussars, 2-0 in London.

178-179. "Rioters" give 'A' Squadron some realistic training at Paderborn prior to a tour of duty in Northern Ireland.

180. 3 July 1982. The regiment is presented with a new Guidon by the Colonel-in-Chief HRH The Princess Margaret. The photograph shows the Guidon being marched past at the head of the regiment. The Guidon Party consists of RSM John Christian, SSGT 'Paddy' O'Neill, WO2 Mick Power and SSGT 'Fred' Longstaff.

181. 'A' Squadron (Close Recce) Scimitars preparing for a days firing on Holme Ranges, 1982.

182. 1st Troop 'C' Squadron Scorpion on Exercise 'Eternal Triangle', 1983.

183. Sergeant George Cleary and Corporal 'Monty' Ford were winners of the 1983 machine gun pairs final in the regimental skill at arms competition.

184. 'C' Squadron 'Boot' Troop prepare to make an assault on Exercise 'Hessian Charge', July 1983.

187. Trooper Longworth and Corporal Davies with a support Saracen, photographed in 1985 when they were attached to the British Aerospace ATGW demonstration team.

188. 10 May 1986. HRH The Princess Margaret with the Lord Mayor of Newcastle-upon-Tyne, Councillor Roy Burgess; and Brigadier J R D Sharpe CBE, at the regiment's Freedom of the City parade.

189. Detmold, 1st June 1989, HRH The Princess Margaret inspecting the regiment. In attendance are Lieutenant D B Curran; Major S R Edwards, 'D' Squadron leader; and Lieutenant-Colonel T D Gregg the commanding officer.

190. HRH The Princess Margaret presenting long service and good conduct medals to Sergeant R Parry, Lance-Corporal 'Zoony' Lewer, Sergeant J McGourley and Sergeant L A Beard.

191. Life can be a bit of a drag at times. Detmold, 1st June 1989.

192. The Colonel in Chief's mounted escort. Corporal J Brookes, Captain M R Good and Lance-Corporal D Beaumont.

193. Second Lieutenant F E V Chubb with the regimental Guidon

194. Guidon bearer and escort. SSGT J W Tervit, WO2 C C McDonald, SSGT R Tervit and RSM P Milnes.

195. Detmold, 1st June 1989. Major J F Walls (retd) on parade with the regimental association members.

196. Miss Emma Ford, daughter of Corporal R M Ford, presenting a bouquet to HRH The Princess Margaret. On the left is Colonel R A Coxwell-Rogers the Colonel of the Regiment, and on the right is Lieutenant-Colonel T D Gregg the commanding officer.

197. The regimental band conducted by bandmaster WOI C J Gould, Detmold, 1st June 1989.

15th/19th The King's Royal Hussars
Record of locations 1922-86

Year	Country	Location	Detachments	Remarks
1922	England	Tidworth (Assaye Bks)		Amalgamation of the 15th King's Hussars & 19th Royal Hussars. Army Order No. 133 11 Apr 1922.
1923	England	Tidworth		
1924-28	Egypt	Helmieh Abbassia	Sidi Bishr Mena Camp Helwan Helwan Camp Wadi Natrun Mena Camp	Left Tidworth Jan 11 for Egypt. Disembarked 25 Jan Port Said. ASSAYE DAY celebrated for first time by 15/19H. Queen Alexandra Colonel in Chief 19H died 21 Nov 1925. Regiment moved from Helmieh to Abbassia 14 Dec 1926. Relieved 9th Lancers. 'B' Sqn disbanded. Machine Gun Sqn formed. 1927. Oct 20th 1928 regiment moved from Egypt to India. Route from Bombay to Risalpur 1,400 miles, Surat, Baroda, Agra, Delhi, Ambala, Lahore, Rawalpindi, reaching Risalpur Nov 14 1928.
1928-33	India	Risalpur	Khanspur, Arbi-Kali, Akora Akora, Peshawar, Charsadda, Shabkadr, Shcik Mohomadi, Utmanzai, Bara Fort Tulandi, Utmanzai, Jinda Khwar, Jalala, Jehangira, Hoti Mardan Charsadda Khanspur Swabbi Rashkai Lahore Kohat Jaganath Jalbai	Called out to assist civil power during disturbances in the Peshawar District. 1930. 'Esla' Day first celebrated. Regiment called out to quell the Red Shirt troubles. 1931. The King approved that the designation of 15th/19th Hussars be changed to 15th The King's Royal Hussars Army Order 177, 1932. Title changed to 15th/19th The King's Royal Hussars. Army Order 207 dtd 21 Dec 1933.
1934	India England	Risalpur Shorncliffe		Jan 15 embarked for England.
1935	England	Shorncliffe		Moved from Shorncliffe to Tidworth Nov 1935.
1936	England	Tidworth		Moved from Tidworth to York Oct 23rd 1936.
1936-38	England	York		Training for mechanisation. Last of the horses left April 1938.
1939	England France	York La Plaisance Monchy-Breton Perenchies Bethune	Binnington Haisnes Douvrin Wattrelos	Regiment equipped with Dragons Tanks, Cardon Lloyds, Austins, Bren Gun Carriers & WT Trucks. Mobilised 1 Sep 1939. Divisional Cavalry 3rd Div Embarked 2nd Oct. Sailed for France 3rd Oct. Disembarked St. Nazaire 4th October.
1940	France Belgium France England	Cambrin Vermelles Cuinchy Annequinn Lannoy Louvain Bovington Rowmarsh Uttoxeter Rushden	Toufflers Roubaix Wattrelds Festubert	9th May 1940. Germany invaded Belgium. 10th May 1940. Regiment in action. 30th May 1940. Evacuated from Dunkirk. Killed in action – 7 Officers, 27 ORs POW – 6 Officers, 100 ORs. 9th Armoured Div 19th Nov 1940.
1941	England	Rushden		
1942	England	Rushden Bury St. Edmonds Brandon Rothbury	Easton on the Hill Livermere Culford Nunnykirk Cragside	
1943	England	Rothbury Duncombe Pk Shakers Wood Nr Thetford, Whitby		

Year	Country	Location	Detachments	Remarks
1944	England	Northumberland	Acton House Swarland Longframlington Weldon Bridge	
		Great Yarmouth Fornham Park Bury St. Edmonds	Fritton	79 Armoured Div.
	France	Arromanches In action Normandy		Sailed 14 Aug 1944. 11 Armoured Div. (159 Inf Bde). Equipped with Cromwell & Comet Tanks. 27 Aug 1944 crossed the Seine.
	Belgium	In action		17 Sep. Crossed into Belgium.
	Holland	In action		
1945	Holland	In action		
	Germany	In action		24 Feb crossed into Germany.
		Occupation	Kappeln Sandbech Buckhagen Arnis	Left Germany 10 Sep 1945.
	Belgium	Ath		Left Ath 10 Oct 1945 for the Canal Zone.
	Egypt	CanalZone Quassasin Gineifa		Join 3rd Infantry Div.
	Palestine	Muquebila	Camp 87	Security duties.
1946	Palestine	Muquebila	Camp 87 Camp 183 (Nr Haifa)	
1947	Egypt	CanalZone		
	Palestine	Gedera		Security duties. 3rd Inf Div disbanded Spring 1947. 1st Inf Div.
	Egypt	Quassasin		'C' Sqn remain in Egypt to run down.
	Sudan	Khartoum		
1948-49	Sudan	Khartoum		1939-45 War Memorial Gong consecrated.
	England	Gosport		
	Germany	Lubeck		Oct 1949.
1950-51	Germany	Lubeck Rhalstedt Hamburg Neumunster		
1952	Germany	Neumunster		
1953	Germany	Neumunster Wesendorf		Joined 7 Armoured Div.
1954	Germany	Wesendorf		Regiment left Germany 4 May 1954.
	England	Colchester		
	Singapore	Selarang Bks Changi		Depart UK on *Empire Clyde* Arrive Singapore 11 July 1954.
	Malaya	Ipoh	Raub Taiping Kulim Cameron Highlands Bikam Kuantan Sungei Siput	26 Aug 1954 took up operational commitment from 12 Lancers.
1955	Malaya	Ipoh	Raub Taiping Kulim Cameron Highlands Bikam Kuantan Sungei Siput	Baling Talks (Ching Peng Communist Terrorist Leader).
1956	Malaya	Ipoh	Sungei Siput Kuala Lumpur	
1957	Malaya	Ipoh	Kuala Lumpur	Embarked Singapore on *Empire Orwell* 4 June 1957. Disembarked
	Singapore		Aden	Southampton 6 July 1957. 'A' Sqn remain in Aden.
	N. Ireland	Omagh	Castle Archdale	Internal Security.
1958	N. Ireland	Omagh	Castle Archdale	Internal Security. 'A' Sqn rejoined regiment from Aden Jan 1958. HRH Princess Margaret appointed Colonel in Chief 28 Oct 1958.
1959	N. Ireland	Omagh	Castle Archdale	Internal Security.
	England		Hadrian's Camp Carlisle	RAC Trg Regt 12 June 59. Bi-Centenary Sep 26 1959. New Guidon presented by HRH Princess Margaret.
	England	Barnard Castle		
1960	England	Barnard Castle		RAC Trg Regiment.
1961	England	Barnard Castle		RAC Trg Regiment.
	Germany	Munster		Regiment moved to Germany 4 Nov 1961.

Year	Country	Location	Detachments	Remarks
1962-66	Germany	Munster		HRH Princess Margaret visited Regiment 26 March 1963. Regiment win Army Inter Unit Boxing Championship by beating the Argyll & Sutherland Highlanders. 1 April 1965 Regiment became an Armoured Regiment after a nineteen year period as an Armoured Car Regiment.
1967	Germany Libya	Munster	Berlin Ras el Aleba Timini Derna El Adem	17 June 1967 'A' Sqn moved to Berlin. 28 Apr 1967 'B' Sqn to Libya for one month. 22 May 1967 'C' Sqn to Libya for 1 month.
	Malta			
1968	Germany England	Munster Tidworth (Bhurtpore Bks)	Warminster	Regiment in UK Station on 25 Jan 1968. 14 June 1968 HRH Princess Margaret visited the Regiment
	Hong Kong	New Territories	Pokok Secong	'C' Sqn Hong Kong Aug/Sep 1968.
1969	England Hong Kong Germany	Tidworth New Territories Fallingbostel	Warminster Secong	'A' Sqn 6 weeks in Hong Kong late summer 1969.
1970	Germany	Fallingbostel		Regiment converts from Centurion tanks to Chieftain tanks 3rd Div Armoured Regiment, 'Swingfire' Troop formed.
1971	Germany N. Ireland	Fallingbostel Long Kesh	Lurgan	July-December 1971 six months operational duties N. Ireland. 'B' Sqn remained in Fallingbostel (The Guard).
1972-73	Germany	Fallingbostel		6/7 June 1972 HRH Princess Margaret visited regiment. HRH Princess Margaret receives the Freedom of the City of Newcastle-upon-Tyne on the regiment's behalf 12th May 1973. 'A' & 'C' Sqns security duties N. Ireland Jan-Apr 1973. Lcpl Stuart awarded the Military Medal for Gallantry in N. Ireland.
	N. Ireland		Gosford Castle Sion Mills Aughnacloy Dungannon Long Kesh Lurgan Portadown	
	Canada		Suffield	RHQ & 'B' Sqn Suffield Training area.
1974	Germany Canada N. Ireland	Fallingbostel Omagh	Suffield St. Angelo Castlederg Belleek Grayvale Kinawley Belcoo Lisnaskea Cookstown Deanery	June 1974 to Aug 74 RHQ 'A', 'C' & HQ Sqns to Suffield Trg area. 19 Nov 1974 Regiment commence operational roll N. Ireland.
1975-76	N. Ireland England Cyprus	Omagh Tidworth	Deanery Episkopi Akrotiri Nicosia Larnaca Skouriotissa Dhekalia Ayios Nicoloas	17 May 1976 Regiment in location at Tidworth. 16 June 1976 'C' Sqn to Cyprus – Sovereign Based. 16 Sep 1976 'B' Sqn to Cyprus – United Nations Force. 13 July 1976 HRH Princess Margaret visited regiment at Tidworth. 11 Nov 1976 HRH Princess Margaret visted 'C' Sqn Cyprus.
1977	England Cyprus	Tidworth	Episkopi Akrotiri Nicosia Larnaca Skouriotissa Dhekalia Ayios Nicoloas	11 March 1977 'A' Sqn Cyprus. 'B' Sqn return to Tidworth. Sep 1977 'A' Sqn depart Cyprus. 22 Nov 1977 'C' Sqn depart Cyprus. 17 Sep 1977 the Regiment & Northumberland Hussars Exercise the Freedom of the City of Newcastle-upon-Tyne.
	Germany	Paderborn		20 Oct 1977 Regiment move to Germany.
1978	Germany N. Ireland	Paderborn	Belleek Belfast Rosslea	1st, 3rd & 5th Troop 'A' Sqn N. Ireland. 2nd Tp 'A' Sqn Canada.
	Canada		Suffield	
1979	Germany N. Ireland Canada	Paderborn	Belleek Suffield	1st & 5th Troop 'A' Sqn Canada. 2nd Troop 'A' Sqn N. Ireland.
1980	Germany	Paderborn		20th March 1980 HRH Princess Margaret visited the regiment.

Year	Country	Location	Detachments	Remarks
1981	Germany	Paderborn		
	Canada		Suffield	3rd & 4th Troop 'A' Sqn Canada Jun-Aug.
	Australia		Engorra	'C' Sqn Australia.
			Shoalwater Bay	
1982	Germany	Paderborn		Presentation of new Guidon by HRH Princess Margaret 3rd July 1982.
	N. Ireland		The Maze	
	Canada		Suffield	
1983	Germany	Paderborn		
	Canada		Suffield	5th Troop 'A' Sqn Canada August.
1984	Germany	Paderborn		
	N. Ireland		The Maze	'A' Sqn Northern Ireland May-July 1984.
			Crumlin Road	
			Portadown	
	Cyprus	Episkopi	Pergamos	'A' Sqn Sovereign Base Cyprus.
			Ayios Nikolaos	
	England	Bovington	Lulworth	Regiment less 'A' Sqn move to Bovington Oct 1984.
1985	England	Bovington	Lulworth	
	Cyprus	Episkopi	Pergamos	
			Ayios Nikoloas	
1986	England	Bovington	Lulworth	May 10th Freedom Parade Newcastle-upon-Tyne.
	Cyprus	Episkopi	Pergamos	
			Ayios Nikoloas	
	Germany			

Battle Honours
15th The King's Hussars
"Emsdorf," "Villers-en-Couche," "Willems," "Egmont-op-Zee," "Sahagun," "Vittoria," "Peninsula," "Waterloo" "Afghanistan," 1878-80."

The Great War–"Mons," "Retreat from Mons," "Marne, 1914," "Aisne, 1924," "Ypres, 1914, '15," "Langemark, 1914," "Gheluvelt," "Nonne Bosschen," "Frezenberg," "Bellewaarde," "Somme, 1916, '18," "Flers-Courcelette," "Cambrai, 1917, '18," "St. Quentin," "Rosieres,", "Amiens," "Albert, 1918," "Bapaume, 1918," "Hindenberg Line," "St. Quentin Canal," "Beaurevoir," "Pursuit to Mons," "France and Flanders, 1914-18."

19th Royal Hussars
"Mysore," "Seringapatam," "Niagara," "Tel-el-Kebir," "Egypt, 1882, '84," "Abu Klea," "Nile, 1884-85," "Defence of Ladysmith," "South Africa, 1899-1902."

The Great War–"Le Cateau," "Retreat from Mons," "Marne, 1914," "Aisne, 1914," "Armentieres, 1914," "Ypres, 1915," "Frezenburg," "Bellewaarde," "Somme, 1916, '18," "Flers-Courcelette," "Cambrai, 1917, '18," "St. Quentin," "Rosieres," "Amiens," "Albert, 1918," "Bapaume, 1918," "Hindenberg Line," "St. Quentin Canal," "Beaurevoir," "Pursuit to Mons," "France and Flanders, 1914-18."

15th/19th The King's Royal Hussars
The Second World War–"Withdrawal to Escaut," "Seine, 1944," "Hechtel," "Nederrijn," "Venraij," "Rhineland," "Hochwald," "Rhine," "Ibbenburen," "Aller," "North-West Europe, 1940, '44-'45."

The Battle Honours in darker print are carried on the Guidon.

AFFILIATED TERRITORIAL REGIMENT
The Northumberland Hussars

ALLIED REGIMENTS
The South Alberta Light Horse (Canadian Army)
1st/15th Royal New South Wales Lancers (Australian Army)
19th Lancers (Pakistan Army)

198. Security patrol by 'B' Squadron during the visit of UN Secretary General Dr Waldheim to Cyprus. In the lead car are Lance-Corporal Stirman and Trooper Connolly, whilst in the second car are Lance-Corporal Hoyle and Trooper McCarroll.